LAKELAND
A TASTE TO REMEMBER

A fine winter's day on Ullswater. It was on the shores of this lake that Wordsworth noticed 'a host of golden daffodils'. (Walt Unsworth)

2

LAKELAND

A TASTE TO REMEMBER

A COLLECTION OF TRADITIONAL LAKELAND TEA RECIPES

by MAVIS DOWNING

CICERONE

MILNTHORPE CUMBRIA

© Mavis Downing 1985
ISBN 0 902363 59 X
First published 1985
Reprinted 1986
Reprinted (Revised) 1992

Cicerone Press,
2 Police Square, Milnthorpe,
Cumbria. LA7 7PY

All temperatures except where specified
are given in Fahrenheit.

Front cover: Great Gable dominates Wasdale (Walt Unsworth)

A Lakeland tea can be a fantastic experience. With spicy, fruity, tea-breads, gingerbreads, home-made cakes and biscuits, delicious scones warm from the oven and thickly spread with rum butter or damson cheese, apple flans and of course, Cumberland sausage.

I have tried to collect together for you, recipes which have been used in Lakeland for many years. I hope you have great enjoyment in trying them for yourselves.

Mavis Downing,

Creamy Fish Pie

1lb cooked fish
1½oz butter
1oz plain flour
½ pint of milk
salt and pepper
1 tablespoon chopped parsley
squeeze of a lemon
creamed mashed potatoes

Skin and bone the fish and flake finely.

Melt 1oz of butter, stir in the flour and cook over a low heat for a few minutes without browning. Stir in the milk and bring to the boil. Add the seasoning, parsley, lemon juice and the fish, put into an oven dish and cover with mashed potato. Dot with remaining butter and heat in the oven at 375° for about 20 minutes.

***

Potted Char

The Char is confined to the very deep lakes. It is most common in Windermere where it has been a local delicacy for many years. There are numerous recipes but I find this to be the one I prefer. Clean the fish, place in an oven dish and cover with white wine, adding a sliced carrot, onion and a bay leaf. Cook very slowly at a low heat until the fish is tender, about 3 to 4 hours.

Allow to cool, remove the skin and bones. Arrange the fillets in a dish and cover with melted butter, bake at 350° for 30 minutes. Remove from oven and add more melted butter if necessary, fish must be covered. Serve cold.

Windermere is the largest lake in England. Its great depth - some 200 feet - make it a suitable breeding ground for char.
(Walt Unsworth)

Morecambe Bay
Potted Shrimps

These shrimps can be bought ready cooked at Flookburgh, a small village on Morecambe Bay.

½lb cooked shrimps
4oz butter
salt, cayenne pepper and nutmeg

Heat the butter, stir in the shrimps and stir until they are well coated with butter. Add a pinch of salt, cayenne and nutmeg. Put into small dishes and leave until set.

Serve with a salad and brown bread.

***

Foil Baked Salmon Steaks

Salmon are caught either from the River Kent at Kendal or the River Lune at Lancaster.

1½lb of middle-cut steaks
2oz butter
a large pinch of mixed herbs
salt, freshly ground black pepper

Wipe fish and place on a double sheet of buttered foil. Place a piece of butter into the centre-cavity of the fish. Season well, sprinkle with herbs. Wrap the foil loosely around the fish and make a tightly -sealed parcel. Place parcel on a baking sheet and bake at 250° for about 1¼ hours.

Chicken and Leek Pie
with Cheese Pastry

Pastry:-
8oz plain flour
pinch of salt
2oz lard
2oz margarine
cold water to mix
3oz grated cheese

Filling:-
1½lb cooked chicken
12oz leeks
1½oz butter
2oz sliced mushrooms
1oz plain flour
½ pint of milk
¼ pint chicken stock
1 teaspoon salt
a little pepper
1 teaspoon parsley

Make the pastry, sift the flour and salt, rub in the margarine and lard. Mix in the grated cheese. Add just enough water to mix to a firm dough. Chill.

Filling:- Cut the chicken into large pieces. Trim and wash the leeks, slice thinly. Melt half the butter in a pan, add the leeks and cook gently for 5 minutes, add the mushrooms and cook for a further 5 minutes. Remove the leeks and mushrooms and put to one side. Add the remaining butter to the pan, stir in the flour and cook for 1 minute. Remove from the heat and gradually stir in the milk and chicken stock. Season with salt and pepper, add the parsley. Return the saucepan to the heat and bring the sauce to the boil, stirring constantly, until thick. Cook for 2 minutes. Remove from the heat and stir in the chicken, leeks and mushrooms. Pour the mixture into a 2½ pint pie dish. Roll out the pastry on to a floured board making it large enough to cover the dish. Use the pastry trimmings to decorate the top of the pie.

Cook in the centre of the oven at 375° until the pastry is golden brown.

Farmhouse Savoury Loaf

4oz oats
4 tablespoons tomato sauce
1lb minced beef
2 teaspoons thyme
1 finely chopped onion
1 teaspoon salt
pepper
2 beaten eggs

Mix all the ingredients together, bind together with the eggs. Grease and line a 2lb loaf tin. Spoon in the mixture and level the top.

Bake in the centre of the oven for about 1 hour at 400°. The loaf will be firm to the touch when cooked.

***

Savoury Meat Loaf

8oz raw minced beef
4oz raw minced pork
1 onion, chopped
pinch of mixed herbs
salt and pepper
3oz breadcrumbs
6 tablespoons milk
1 beaten egg
2 tablespoons Worcester sauce

Mix together all the ingredients, pack into a well greased 1lb loaf tin.

Bake in the centre of the oven at 375° for 1 hour. When cooked turn out onto a hot dish and serve with a crisp salad and crusty bread.

Also useful cold for picnics.

The Hollows, Borrowdale.
This delectable stretch of mixed woods by the river Derwent near Grange, is renowned for its squirrels which are so bold they entertain the campers and visitors at close quarters. Here in early spring the farmer moves some of his sheep to a new pasture through the woods. (Brian Evans)

Farmhouse Sausage Patties

2lb lean minced lamb or beef
2 teaspoons salt
1 tablespoon ground coriander
1 teaspoon grated nutmeg
12oz fat pork, finely chopped
½ teaspoon ground cloves
½ teaspoon black pepper
lard for frying

Mix together all the ingredients except the lard. Using about 2oz per portion, form the mixture into round patties.

Heat the lard in a large frying pan over a medium heat and fry for about 15-20 minutes, turning occasionally, until cooked through and well browned.

***

Open Meat and Vegetable Pastry

8oz shortcrust pastry
1 sliced onion
a few mushrooms
4 diced cooked carrots
3 skinned chopped tomatoes
½ cup cooked peas
diced cooked meat
vegetable oil
grated cheese

Roll pastry out into a square and place into a round greased sandwich tin.

Heat oil and fry the onions until tender, add mushrooms and cook slowly. Add these to all the other ingredients and mix well. Fill the pastry case, sprinkle with grated cheese, fold the corners over the filling. Brush with beaten egg and bake at 350° for 30 minutes, or until brown.

Farmhouse Loaf

This was made to use up any left-over meat and cold vegetables. It made a sustaining meal for the farm worker without much cost.

Boil 2lbs of potatoes and mash well. Mix in 3oz of margarine and 2oz of plain flour. Bind together with a little milk. Grease a large loaf tin and line the bottom and sides with the potato mix, keeping enough to make a lid to cover. Mince left-over cooked meat, add chopped cooked vegetables and bind together with a little gravy. Pack the mixture into the potato-lined tin, cover with the potato lid. Brush with egg and bake at 350° until golden brown.

***

Lakeland 'Tatie Pot'

2lbs best neck of lamb
2 black puddings
2lbs of sliced potatoes
1 large sliced onion
salt and pepper
¾ pint of water, or stock
small amount of butter (melted)

Trim any excess fat from the meat, slice the black puddings.

In a large casserole, layer the potato, onions, meat and black pudding, season each layer. Finish with a layer of potatoes. Pour over, the water, sprinkle with salt and cover with a lid. Bake in a moderate oven for 1½ hours. Remove the lid and brush the potatoes with the melted butter. Return to the oven for the top layer of potatoes to brown, about 30 minutes.

Serve with pickled red cabbage.

Farmhouse Pork and Rabbit

Serve this delicious dish with jacket potatoes, baked at the same time.

1 rabbit, jointed
8oz boneless pork, finely cubed
head of celery, chopped
2 onions, chopped
½ teaspoon sage
½ teaspoon thyme
9 fluid oz milk
4 fluid oz chicken stock

Coat the rabbit in a seasoned flour, made with 1oz flour salt and pepper.

Put half the celery and onion into a greased casserole dish. Arrange the rabbit portions on to this and then the pork cubes. Sprinkle in the herbs. Cover with the remaining celery and onion. Mix the milk and chicken stock together and pour over the ingredients in the dish. Cover and bake at 325° for 2½ hours.

***

Town End, Troutbeck was once the home of the Browne family. It is now National Trust property and open to the public. (Walt Unsworth)

Cumberland Pork Loaf

2oz stale white breadcrumbs
¼ pint milk
1½lb minced pork
8oz Cumberland sausage meat
1 beaten egg
salt and pepper
chopped parsley
2 bay leaves

Soak the breadcrumbs in the milk.

In a large bowl mix the minced pork, sausage meat, soaked bread-crumbs and beaten egg. Mix well, season with salt and pepper.

Make a Cumberland sauce to cover the bottom of the tin.

4 tablespoons redcurrant jelly
4 tablespoons demerara sugar
finely grated peel of 1 orange
2 tablespoons orange juice
2 teaspoons of 'made' mustard

Blend together.

Spread the sauce over the bottom of a 2lb. loaf tin.

Spoon in the meat mixture and pack down firmly. Put the bay leaves on top.

Cover the tin with foil and bake at 350° for 1 hour. Remove the bay leaves, pour off the juices, and turn out on to a serving dish. Serve the juices in a sauceboat with the meat.

***

Cumberland Sausage

Cumberland sausage is sold all over the Lake District, each butcher making the sausage to his own particular recipe. It is sold and cooked in a continuous strip and therefore requires extra cooking.

The best way to cook Cumberland sausage is in a buttered roasting tin, kept in a fairly tight coil. Prick carefully and bake for ½ hour in a hot oven. Serve with apple sauce.

Cumberland Sausage Loaf

4oz chopped bacon
1 medium onion, chopped
2 large cooking apples diced
1lb Cumberland sausage,
skin removed

½ pint fresh breadcrumbs
2 tablespoons moist brown sugar
2 teaspoons of made mustard
browned breadcrumbs

Grease a 2lb loaf tin and coat bottom and sides with browned crumbs.

Put the bacon into a medium saucepan and cook slowly, when crisp add the onion, cover with the lid and cook for a few minutes. Add the diced apple, cook for a further few minutes until the apple is mushy.

Remove from the heat and add the rest of the ingredients. Mix well.

Pack into the prepared tin, sprinkle more browned crumbs on top.

Bake at 350° fo 50 minutes.

Serve hot, but also excellent cold either for sandwiches or sliced with a salad.

***

Cold Boiled Bacon

A lovely filling for sandwiches, or serve cold with home-made pickles and a green salad.

3lb boned and rolled bacon joint
1 bay leaf
1 chopped stick of celery
1 teaspoon mustard powder
bouquet garni
1 tablespoon clear honey
4 whole black peppercorns

Coating:-
2 tablespoons of made mustard
3oz freshly toasted breadcrumbs

Place the bacon joint in a large saucepan. Cover with cold water, bring to the boil, drain and rinse off any scum.

Cover with fresh water, add all the ingredients and bring to the boil. Simmer for 25 minutes to the pound plus an extra 25 minutes. Keep the saucepan covered during the cooking.

Allow the joint to cool in the liquid.

Strip off the rind. Spread the sides and top with the mustard then roll the joint in the toasted breadcrumbs.

Slice and serve cold.

*The high fells of Lakeland would not be the same
without the ever-present sheep. (Dave Murray)*

Quick Country Flan

Enough slices of thin sliced bread
to cover a 9" flan tin
Butter for bread and about 2oz for cooking
1 chopped onion
4 rashers of bacon, chopped
4oz sliced mushrooms
2 eggs
½ pint of milk
salt and pepper
3oz grated cheese

Butter the bread and press the slices, buttered side up, well down into the bottom of a greased flan tin. Cut the remaining slices in half and line the sides, cut any excess bread off the top.

Melt the 2oz of butter in a pan and cook the onion and bacon for a few minutes until golden brown. Cool.

Place the sliced mushrooms on the bread base. Cover with the onion and mushrooms. Beat the eggs into the milk, season well.

Strain the mixture into the flan case, sprinkle the cheese on the top.

Place the flan tin on a baking sheet and cook at 375° for 40 minutes until set.

Serve warm.

***

Farmhouse Bacon and Egg Pie

As a farmhouse pie was made to suit the size of the family, the quantities of the ingredients were judged by the size of the pie-plate used.

Enough short-crust pastry to line the pie-plate and to form a lid.

Remove rind from bacon and over-lap the rashers on the pastry. Beat 3 eggs well, this is about the correct quantity for the average size pie-plate. Pour eggs over the bacon. Do not season as there will be enough salt in the bacon. Cover with the pastry lid. Brush top with a little beaten egg. Bake at 350° for about 1¼ hours. Delicious hot but also useful for a picnic, cold with a salad.

Riverside Savoury Apple Flan

1 9" flan case, baked blind and cooled
6 lean slices of bacon
2 large cooking apples, peeled, cored and chopped
¾ pint of thick white sauce, warm
6oz grated cheese
1 teaspoon salt
½ teaspoon pepper
1 tablespoon chopped fresh parsley

Place the cooked flan case on an oven-proof plate.

In a frying pan melt 1 tablespoon butter over moderate heat, add the chopped bacon and fry until crisp. Remove bacon from pan and drain on kitchen paper. Add the chopped apple to pan and cook for 5-7 minutes until tender.

Place white sauce in a bowl add the bacon, apples and half of the grated cheese. Season with salt and pepper. Mix well. The cheese will melt in the warm sauce. Pour the mixture in to the flan case. Sprinkle with the rest of the cheese. Place the flan under a hot grill for 5 minutes until the cheese is bubbling. Sprinkle with parsley and serve at once.

***

Apple and Bacon Plate Pie

This is a savoury pie which should be served with pickled red cabbage.

8oz shortcrust
pastry

Filling:-
1 large cooking apple, peeled
8oz bacon rashers
1 onion, thinly sliced
4oz potato, thinly sliced, then blanched for 1 minute
salt and pepper   *½ teaspoon sage*
4 teaspoons of light ale

Roll out pastry on a floured board and divide in half. Line andgrease 9" pie-plate.

Core and slice the apple, cut the bacon rashers into quarters. Make a layer each of bacon, onion, apple and potato in the pastry lined pie-plate. Season with salt and pepper and sprinkle over the sage. Spoon over the light ale.

Cover the pie with the remaining pastry. Cut a stream vent in the top and brush with either egg or milk to glaze.

Bake at 400° for 50 minutes, serve hot.

Evening light on the Wastwater Screes. (Walt Unsworth)

Roast Venison

A traditional Lakeland dish, always served with red cabbage. A haunch of venison is the best joint to roast.

Make a marinade of ½ pint red wine, ½ pint vinegar, 1 sliced onion, pinch of parsley, thyme and a bay leaf.

Put the venison in the marinade to soak for two days, turning the meat occasionally. When ready to cook the meat, put the joint on a rack in a roasting tin with the marinade. Cook at 375° until the meat is tender, 15-20 minutes per 1lb, baste frequently with the marinade.

When cooked, strain juices from pan and thicken to serve.

***

Venison Stew

Use meat from the shoulder and neck which is slightly tough and is best for stews. Cut into 1 inch cubes and marinate.

2lb of venison	*Marinade*
½lb streaky bacon	*½ pint red wine*
2oz butter	*½ pint vinegar*
2 onions	*1 sliced onion*
3 level tablespoons plain flour	*pinch of parsley, thyme*
	1 bay leaf
½ pint red wine	
1 clove garlic	
salt and pepper	
1 teaspoon mixed herbs	

Mix marinade and steep the meat for 4 hours. Drain thoroughly.

Chop bacon and fry gently in an iron casserole or heavy based saucepan, add butter, chopped onions, cook until transparent. Sprinkle in the flour and let this roux brown, stirring all the time. Add the venison. Cook until brown stirring, mix in crushed garlic and herbs and cover with the red wine. Cover tightly with lid and simmer for 3 hours.

Red Cabbage

1 red cabbage, shredded

In a saucepan with a tight fitting lid, put ½″ of water and white wine vinegar mixed in equal parts, add salt, pepper, 1 tablespoon butter and 1 dessertspoon brown sugar.

Add cabbage and cook for a few minutes. Do not overcook. Strain and serve with venison.

***

Easter Ledge Pudding

Easter Ledge is another name for 'Polygonum bistorta'.

½lb Easter Ledges	*1 teacupful of barley*
½lb young nettle tops	*½ teaspoon salt*
1 large onion	

Remove the stems from the Easter Ledges and chop finely with the young nettles and the onion. Wash the barley and sprinkle this amongst the greens with the salt. Put the mixture into a muslin bag and boil for two hours. When cooked beat 1 egg and a little butter into the greens. Season with salt and pepper. This can be eaten as a vegetable or fried with bacon.

***

Farmhouse Vegetable Grill

Serve this creamy, crispy vegetable dish with boiled ham or beef.

¾lb carrots	*2 tablespoons horseradish sauce*
½lb swedes	*salt*
½lb parsnips	*black pepper*
1½lb potatoes	*3oz grated cheese*
¼ pint of milk	*1oz bread crumbs*
2oz butter	

Prepare the vegetables and cut into 1 inch cubes. Boil together for about 25 minutes, until tender. Drain and mash with the milk and half the butter. Add the horseradish and season with the salt and pepper. Put the mixture into a greased ovenproof dish. Mix the crumbs and cheese together and sprinkle on top of the vegetables. Dot with cubes of the remaining butter and brown under a hot grill. Serve piping hot.

Vegetable Bake

1lb finely shredded cabbage
½lb finely sliced onion
4oz grated carrot
pepper and salt
¼ pint water
2oz margarine
1lb of cooked mashed potato
4oz grated cheese
chopped parsley

Mix the cabbage, onion, carrot, salt and pepper and place them in a greased 2 pint dish. Add the water and margarine. Cover with the mashed potato and sprinkle with the cheese.

Bake at 400° until the cabbage is tender, about 40 minutes. The top will be golden brown.

Serve with Cumberland sausage which can be baked at the same time.

***

Cheese Delight

A very inexpensive dish which was quickly made. Used as a 'filler' if there wasn't enough meat.

Spread 2oz of butter thickly over the bottom of an oven dish. Sprinkle a layer of finely chopped onion over the butter and then cover with 8oz of, grated cheese. Beat up 4 eggs lightly with a little salt and pepper. Pour this over the cheese, bake at 400° for 15-20 minutes. Serve with a jacket potato or just on its own.

Grasmere seen from the popular Loughrigg Terrace.
(Walt Unsworth)

Onion and Cheese Flan

Line a flan tin with shortcrust pastry. Make a filling with ¾ pint of thick white sauce, add a cupful of chopped boiled onions, 2oz grated cheese, 1 tablespoon of chopped fresh parsley, season well.

Pour into the lined flan tin, garnish with slices of tomato and sprinkle with a little grated cheese on top.

Bake for 35 minutes at 350°.

This flan will reheat without spoiling.

***

Farmhouse Scones with Cheese

8oz plain flour
1 teaspoon cream of tartar
½ teaspoon bicarbonate of soda
2oz butter
3oz grated cheese
salt and pepper
½ teaspoon dry mustard powder
¼ pint of milk

Sieve the flour, cream of tartar and the bicarbonate of soda. Rub in the butter, add the cheese, salt and pepper. Mix with enough milk to give a soft dough.

Turn out on to a floured board, roll out to ¾ ″ thick. Cut into two large circles. Mark in triangles. Glaze with milk. Put on to a greased baking sheet and bake at 425° for about 10-15 minutes.

Serve warm with lots of butter.

Supper Loaf

8oz S.R. flour
1 teaspoon baking powder
3 teaspoons mustard powder
¼ teaspoon salt
¼ teaspoon pepper
2oz butter
4 rashers bacon, chopped
1 egg
4oz grated cheese
¼ pint of milk

Mix all the ingredients, except for 1oz of the cheese, in a large bowl. Mix well together. Grease a 2lb loaf tin and spoon in the mixture. Sprinkle with the 1oz cheese. Bake at 375° for 45 minutes. Cool in the tin for 10 minutes before turning out.

Slice and spread with butter.

***

Cheese and Walnut Loaf

8oz S.R. flour
1 teaspoon dry mustard powder
1 teaspoon salt
pinch of pepper
3oz butter
4oz grated cheese
1oz walnuts, chopped
2 eggs
¼ pint of milk

Sift the flour, mustard, salt and pepper into a mixing bowl. Rub in the butter until the mixture resembles fine breadcrumbs.

Stir in the grated cheese and the walnuts. Beat the eggs and milk together, add to the dry ingredients and mix to a soft dropping consistency. Grease a 1lb loaf tin, spoon in the mixture and smooth the top.

Bake at 350° for ¾-1hour until golden brown.

The crumpled crest of Haystacks dominate the head of Buttermere, with Scarth Gap, the path over to Ennerdale, on the right. (Dave Murray)

Cheese and Herb Loaf

3oz grated cheese
8oz S.R. flour
½ teaspoon salt
1 teaspoon dry mustard
½ teaspoon mixed dried herbs
1 egg
¼ pint milk
1oz of melted butter

Place grated cheese in bowl, add sifted flour, salt, mustard and herbs.

Beat egg into milk and add to flour mixture, mix well.

Place in a well greased 1lb loaf tin. Bake in a moderate oven, 350° for 50 mins.

Allow to cool for 5 minutes in tin before turning out.

***

Soda Bread

This traditional recipe is surprisingly easy to make. Serve warm with butter and home-made jam for tea.

1lb plain flour
1 teaspoon bicarbonate of soda
1 teaspoon salt
4 to 8 fluid oz milk

Sift the flour, soda and salt into a large mixing bowl. With a wooden spoon gradually beat in 4 fluid oz of milk. The dough should be smooth but firm. If necessary, add more milk.

Put the dough onto a floured board and shape it into a flat round loaf. Place on to a greased baking sheet, with a sharp knife, cut a deep cross on top of the loaf.

Bake at 425° for 30-35 minutes, or until golden brown.

The River Derwent at Grange. Behind is Goat Crag on a shoulder of the oddly named fell High Spy. (Brian Evans)

Coniston Loaf

15oz wheatmeal flour
3oz strong white flour
1 well heaped teaspoon baking-powder
2 teaspoons salt
1 egg
2 tablespoons vinegar
1½ cups of milk

Sift the flour, baking-powder and salt together into a large mixing bowl. Beat the egg and vinegar together. Mix the egg and vinegar into the flour and use the milk to make a stiff dough. Grease a 2lb loaf tin and place in the dough.

Bake for about 20 minutes at 425°. The loaf should sound hollow when tapped on the base. Eat within 3 to 4 days.

***

Fruity Tea Bread

1lb sultanas
1lb raisins
1lb soft brown sugar
15 fluid oz of strong black tea
1lb plain flour
3 eggs, beaten
1 tablespoon baking powder
1 tablespoon mixed spice
3 tablespoons honey, warmed to glaze

Put fruit, sugar and tea into a large bowl to soak overnight.

Heat oven to 325°, brush 3 ½lb loaf tins with margarine and dust with flour.

Add flour and eggs alternately to the tea and fruit mixture, add the baking powder and spice and mix well.

Divide between the 3 tins and level off. Cook for 1½ hours. Test in centre of loaf with a skewer. Allow to cool for 5 minutes in tin before turning out. When cold, warm the honey, brush over the tops and leave to set.

Rich Tea Bread

¼ teaspoon bicarbonate of soda
10oz S.R. flour
4oz soft dark brown sugar
6oz sultanas
2oz chopped peel
½ teaspoon ground ginger
¼ teaspoon mixed spice
pinch of salt
6oz black treacle
3 tablespoons milk
1 beaten egg

Mix all the dry ingredients in a bowl. Dissolve the bicarbonate of soda in a little of the milk. Warm gently the rest of the milk with the treacle. Remove pan from the heat, add the beaten egg and the bicarbonate of soda - milk mix. Pour this liquid onto the dry ingredients and mix well. Pour into a well greased 2lb loaf tin and bake for the first 30 minutes at 350° then for 50-60 minutes at 325°. Leave in tin to cool. Serve sliced with butter.

***

Cumberland Bun Loaf

1lb plain flour
¼lb margarine
6oz sugar
4oz currants
2oz mixed peel
1 tablespoon syrup
½ teaspoon nutmeg
1 teaspoon bicarbonate of soda
1 tablespoon vinegar
½ pint of milk

Rub the margarine into the flour, mix in the sugar, currants, peel, nutmeg, syrup and vinegar. Dissolve the soda in the milk, add to the mixture and mix quickly. Put into a well greased 2lb loaf tin. Bake at 325° for 2½-3 hours.

Walnut-Topped Apple Loaf

4oz softened butter
4oz soft brown sugar
2 eggs
1oz walnuts, chopped
1 large eating apple, with peel, grated
1 orange
4oz S.R. flour
1 teaspoon ground cinnamon
¼ teaspoon ground cloves
4oz wheatmeal flour
1 oz raisins

Cream the butter and sugar, add the eggs and beat well. Finely grate the orange rind. Sift the flours with the spices. Stir into the creamed mixture, the walnuts, apple, orange rind and raisins, add the flour and three tablespoons of the orange juice. Place mixture into a 2lb loaf tin, well greased and paper lined. Bake at 350° for 1 hour.

Topping:
1½oz walnut halves
1oz butter
2oz brown sugar

Melt butter in pan with sugar, brush top of cake. Place cake under a medium grill for about 30 seconds until the topping bubbles. Place the walnuts over the cake. Turn out the cake and leave to cool.

***

Aira Force near Ullswater is one of Lakeland's best known waterfalls.
(Walt Unsworth)

Border Treacle Loaf

4oz melted butter
4 fluid oz black treacle
2 eggs, beaten
8oz plain flour
1½ teaspoons baking powder
1½ teaspoons ground ginger
½ teaspoon allspice
¼ teaspoon ground cinnamon
¼ teaspoon salt
4oz rolled oats
5 fluid oz sour cream
4 tablespoons sultanas
2 tablespoons chopped walnuts

In a mixing bowl, mix the butter, treacle and eggs together with a fork until they are well blended.

Sift the flour and the baking powder into a bowl, add the spices, salt and oats. Stir until mixed. Gradually add the butter and treacle mixture into the flour mixture, beating well. Stir in the sour cream, then fold in the sultanas and walnuts.

Grease a 1½lb loaf tin. Spoon the batter into the tin and bake at 350° for 1 hour. Allow to cool in the tin for 10 minutes before removing. Serve either warm or cold, sliced and spread with butter.

***

Date and Banana Loaf

3oz margarine
4oz caster sugar
7oz S.R. flour
4oz chopped dates
2oz chopped walnuts
1 large egg
¼ teaspoon salt
¼ teaspoon bicarbonate of soda
2 ripe mashed bananas

Beat the margarine and sugar until creamy. Add the egg, and stir in the rest of the ingredients. Grease a 1lb loaf tin, spoon in the mixture and bake at 350° for 50-60 minutes. It should be firm to the touch when cooked. Leave in tin to cool for 5 minutes.

***

Mother's Bread Pudding

12oz stale white bread, in small pieces
18 fluid oz warm water
6oz sultanas
4oz raisins
2oz currants
4oz soft brown sugar
2 beaten eggs
5 fluid oz milk
1 teaspoon grated nutmeg
1 teaspoon ground cinnamon
½ teaspoon ground ginger
small amount caster sugar

Place the bread in a large mixing bowl, pour over the water and leave to soak for 2 hours. Pour off any excess water.

Mash bread with a fork until smooth, mix in dried fruits and brown sugar. Add eggs, milk, spices and stir until well mixed.

Grease an 8″ baking tin, spoon in the mixture and bake at 325° for 1-1½ hours or until a skewer inserted in the centre of the pudding comes out clean. Sprinkle with caster sugar.

The Castlerigg Stone Circle stands 2 miles east of Keswick. It dates from the Bronze Age. (Dave Murray)

Westmorland Oatmeal Apples

8 large cooking apples, peeled and thickly sliced
2 teaspoons ground cinnamon

Topping:
4oz butter, (melted)
4oz rolled oats
4oz soft brown sugar

Spread the sliced apple into a greased ovenproof dish. Sprinkle with the cinnamon.

Mix the rolled oats and sugar together and sprinkle over the apples.

Pour the melted butter over the oats.

Bake at 400° for about 30 minutes, the crust should be slightly brown.

***

Apple and Ginger Pudding

2lbs of cooking apples
1oz sugar
6oz S.R. flour
3oz margarine
2 tablespoons golden syrup
1 teaspoon ground ginger
milk to mix
2 eggs

Peel and core the apples, stew in very little water and sweeten to taste.

Cream the margarine, sugar and syrup together, beat in the eggs, one by one.

Sieve the flour and ginger into the mix, fold in and use a little milk to bring to a dropping consistency.

Place the cooked apples into a pie-dish and cover with the ginger mixture.

Bake at 350° until golden brown.
Serve either hot or cold.

Traditional Bread Pudding

12oz stale white bread, in small pieces
18 fluid oz warm water
6oz raisins
4oz sultanas
4oz soft brown sugar
2 eggs lightly beaten
5 fluid oz milk
½ teaspoon grated nutmeg
½ teaspoon ground ginger

Place the bread in a large mixing bowl. Pour over the water and leave to soak for about 3 hours. Pour off any excess water. Mash the bread with a fork, mix in all the fruit and the brown sugar.

Add the eggs, milk and spices. Mix well. Grease an 8″ square tin, spoon in the mixture. Bake at 325° for 1-1½ hours, or until a skewer inserted into the middle comes out clean.

Sprinkle a little icing sugar over the pudding when removed from the oven.

***

Gooseberry Summer Pudding

2lb gooseberries
1 tablespoon water
8 thin slices of white bread with crusts removed
6oz caster sugar
1½lb pudding basin

Clean the gooseberries, put in a saucepan with the water, cover and cook gently until tender, about 10 minutes. Leave to cool.

Line the pudding basin with the bread, putting one slice on the bottom and six slices around the sides, slightly overlapping. Mix the sugar into the gooseberries and spoon the mixture into the basin. Place the last slice of bread on the top. Cover with a plate and stand a heavy weight on the top. Leave overnight. Chill.

Any soft fruits can be used in the same way, just alter the sugar and sweeten to taste.

Clipping Time Pudding

This was a traditional pudding always made at clipping time, taken out to the shearers by the ladies of the house. It was served spread with bone-marrow. Butter is a good substitute.

4oz rice

1 pint of milk

3oz sugar

1 teaspoon ground cinnamon

1 beaten egg

4oz currants

4oz raisins

1 tablespoon butter

pinch of salt

Blanch the rice in a little boiling salted water. Strain, then cook it slowly in the milk. Add the sugar and cinnamon, mix well and bring to the boil, cook gently until the rice is soft. Add the beaten egg, fruit and stir well, add the butter and season. Put into an ovenproof dish and bake at 400° for about 20 minutes. Serve cut into wedges spread with butter.

***

Rhubarb with Oatmeal Crumble

2lbs of rhubarb,	*Crumble*
cut into 1 inch pieces	*4oz flour*
1½oz sugar	*2oz butter*
	1½oz sugar
	1oz demerara sugar
	3 tablespoons oatmeal

Put the rhubarb into an ovenproof dish and sprinkle with the sugar.

Make the topping by rubbing the butter into the flour until it resembles breadcrumbs. Add the sugar, mix together.

Put this mixture over the rhubarb.

Mix together the oatmeal and demerara and sprinkle over the top.

Bake at 400° for 45 minutes until the crumble is golden brown.

The Eskdale Hunt out for the day. Lakeland fox hunting is done on foot across the wild fells. (Brian Evans)

John Peel Tart

Shortcrust pastry case
Filling:-
6oz currants
1 oz mixed peel
1oz butter
1oz ground almonds
4oz syrup
2 tablespoons rum butter
½ teaspoon mixed spice
1 teaspoon lemon juice

Line a greased swiss-roll tin with pastry. Warm the syrup and butter, stir in the rest of the ingredients and allow to cool. Spread on to the pastry and cover with a pastry lid. Bake for 40 minutes at 380°. When cold sprinkle with caster sugar.

***

Creamy Apple Tart

Pastry	*Topping*
9oz plain flour	*1½lbs eating apples*
4½oz butter	*1½oz caster sugar*
1 egg beaten	*4 fluid oz double cream*
1oz icing sugar	*3 fluid oz milk*
Pinch salt	*2 eggs*
2 tablespoons milk	*dash of rum*

Make the pastry by sifting the flour and salt, mix in the sifted icing sugar. Cut the butter into the flour and work in quickly into a paste with the egg and milk. Pat the pastry with your hands into a round circle, on a floured board. Leave it in a cool place for ½ hour.

Meanwhile peel, core and then slice the apples very thinly. Butter and flour and large pie dish. Line with the pastry, don't roll it out just press it out to fit the dish with your knuckles. Prick the base with a fork and fill with overlapping slices of apple.

Whisk together the eggs and sugar until fluffy. Whisk in the milk and cream, add rum. Pour this mixture over the apples and bake at 360°F until golden brown on top.

Farmhouse Treacle Tart

Filling:-

1 teacupful golden syrup

1½ teacups breadcrumbs

juice and grated rind of 1 small lemon

Enough flaky pastry to line a greased swiss-roll tin

Prepare the pastry and chill well.

Mix the syrup with the breadcrumbs and the rind and juice of the lemon.

Roll out the pastry and cut in two. Roll one piece rather thinner than the other and use to line the swiss-roll tin.

Spread with the syrup mixture. Place the second piece of pastry over and seal the edges. Bake at 400° for 30-40 minutes. Just before it is finished, remove from the oven and brush with a little beaten egg white.

Dust at once with caster sugar and return to the oven for 2 or 3 minutes to frost the top. Leave to cool then cut into squares to serve.

***

Harvest Apple Pie

8oz shortcrust pastry

2lb cooking apples, cooked in a little water

mincemeat

beaten egg for glazing

caster sugar

Roll out pastry to make enough to line an 8″ round pie plate and a lid to cover.

Spread pastry with a layer of mincemeat and cover this with cooked apple.

At this point, if you have it to spare, you can sprinkle a tablespoon of rum on to the mixture.

Cover with pastry lid and glaze with the beaten egg, sprinkle with caster sugar. Bake at 375° for about 35 minutes, until golden brown.

Serve with fresh cream.

Winter morning in Langdale. (Walt Unsworth)

Border Tart

Pastry:-	Filling:-
6oz plain flour	2oz margarine
pinch of salt	2oz caster sugar
1½oz lard	1 egg
1½oz margarine	2oz currants
cold water to mix	1oz ground almonds
	almond essence

Icing:-
3oz icing sugar
2 teaspoons lemon juice

Make pastry by sifting flour with the salt, rub in margarine and lard until mixture resembles breadcrumbs. Use enough cold water to make a firm dough.

Line a 9″ flan tin with pastry.

To make the filling:- Beat the butter and sugar to a soft cream, beat in the egg and add the currants. Mix in the ground almonds and a few drops of almond essence. Put the mixture onto the pastry and smooth over. Roll scraps of pastry quite thinly and cut into strips about ¼″ wide. Lay over the mixture in a trellis pattern.

Bake the tart at 400° for about 15 minutes and then reduce heat to 300° for a further 15 minutes. Allow to cool but ice whilst still warm.

Mix the icing sugar with the lemon juice and a few drops of cold water, spoon over the top of the tart, thinly. Filling and trellis pattern should be seen through the icing.

***

Cheese and Apple Pie

8oz shortcrust pastry
1lb cooking apples, peeled, cored and sliced
2oz brown sugar
pinch of mixed spice
2oz grated cheese

Use half of the pastry to line a greased 8″ sandwich tin.

Spread the sliced apples over the pastry, sprinkle with the sugar, spice and the cheese. Cover with a pastry lid, seal the edges well. Brush the pie with cold water and sprinkle with caster sugar.

Bake at 375°, in the centre of the oven for 1½ hours.

A Westmorland Three-Decker

1½lbs of mixed sliced apple
and blackberries
1lb shortcrust pastry
sugar to taste

Grease and line with greaseproof an 8″ round tin.

Divide the pastry into three, roll one piece into a round to fit the tin.

Put half of the fruit onto the pastry and sprinkle with sugar, cover with another layer of pastry and then the remaining fruit and sugar. Cover with the remaining pastry. Brush with cold water and sprinkle with caster sugar.

Bake at 375° for 1 hour.

Serve warm with custard or fresh cream.

***

Treacle Scones

8oz plain flour
½ teaspoon bicarbonate of soda
1 teaspoon cream of tartar
½ teaspoon mixed spice
½ teaspoon ground cinnamon
large pinch of salt
1oz butter
1 teaspoon sugar
1 tablespoon black treacle
approximately ¼ pint of milk
milk to glaze

Sieve together the flour, bicarbonate of soda, cream of tartar, salt and spices.

Rub in the butter, add the treacle and sugar. Use enough milk to mix to a soft dough. Knead lightly and roll out to about ½″ thick. Cut into rounds, brush tops with milk and bake at 425° for about 12-15 minutes.

Serve with butter and home-made jam.

Ginger and Walnut Scones

½lb plain flour
1 teaspoon baking powder
½ teaspoon salt
2oz margarine

1oz caster sugar
2oz preserved ginger, chopped
1oz chopped walnuts
1 egg
milk to mix

Sieve the dry ingredients and cut and rub in the margarine. Add the sugar, ginger and chopped walnuts. Beat the egg and add a little milk. Use to mix all to a soft dough. Turn on to a floured board, roll out to about 1″ thick. Cut into rounds, brush with egg and bake at 475° for 15 minutes.

***

Drop Scones

8oz plain flour
pinch of salt
2 eggs

2oz caster sugar
1 teaspoon cream of tartar
½ teaspoon bicarbonate of soda
milk

Sieve the flour and salt into a bowl. Make a well in the centre, break in the eggs and add enough milk to make a thickish batter. Stir in the sugar and finally stir in the cream of tartar and bicarbonate of soda. Drop dessertspoonfuls of batter on to a greased pre-heated griddle. A large heavy frying pan can be used. Cook on one side until bubbles begin to burst, then turn over to cook the other side.

Cool between the folds of a tea towel to keep soft. Serve with butter.

***

Date Flapjack

1lb oats
8oz butter
8oz chopped dates

8 heaped teaspoons sugar
2 tablespoons syrup

Melt butter and syrup, mix in oats, sugar and dates. Spread this mixture into a well greased tin, cook for 25-30 minutes at 350°. Cut while still warm.

The tiny 16th century Bridge House is a popular feature of Ambleside. (Walt Unsworth)

Lakeland Slice

4oz butter or margarine
4oz caster sugar
2 eggs
8oz S.R. flour
1 teaspoon mixed spice
10oz of mixed fruit,
made up of chopped cherries,
sultanas, currants etc.
¼ pint milk

Marzipan Paste:
4oz ground almonds
4oz icing sugar
1 egg lightly beaten
(Sieve sugar into bowl,
add almonds and
mix with enough egg to
make a dough)

flaked almonds

Put butter, caster sugar, eggs, flour, spice and fruit juice into a bowl, add milk and beat until creamy. Pour half the mixture into a well greased 8″ or 9″ square tin. Roll out the almond paste the same size and place on top of the mixture. Cover paste with the remaining mix. Sprinkle with almonds. Bake at 350° for 30-40 minutes until golden brown. Cut into slices when cold.

***

Cumberland Rum Nickies

8oz shortcrust pastry
4oz currants
1 tablespoon rum
1 tablespoon soft brown sugar
½ teaspoon ground nutmeg
1oz rum butter
1oz butter

Soak the currants in the rum for about 1 hour. Melt the rum butter and the 1oz of butter in a saucepan. Add the nutmeg and the currant-rum mixture. Leave to stand until cool.

Roll out the pastry, cut into rounds. Stir the currant mixture well and place a large spoonful into the middle of the pastry rounds. Cover with another round and seal the edges well. Prick over the top with a fork. Brush with milk and sprinkle with caster sugar.

Bake at 400° for 10-15 minutes.

Honey and Walnut Bars

4oz sugar
4oz clear honey
4 tablespoons water
2oz cooking chocolate
5oz chopped walnuts
8oz plain flour
1 teaspoon baking-powder
1 teaspoon bicarbonate of soda
½ teaspoon ground cinnamon
2 beaten eggs

In a saucepan, bring the sugar, honey and water to the boil over a low heat, stirring. Remove from the heat and stir in the chocolate and the walnuts. Continue to stir until the chocolate has melted. Allow to cool.

Sift the flour, baking-powder, bicarbonate of soda and cinnamon. Stir in the chocolate and honey mixture. Beat in the eggs and blend well.

Turn into a greased 10" x 14" baking tin. Bake at 350° for 35 minutes.

Remove from the oven and while the cake is hot cut into bars. Leave to go cold before removing from the tin.

***

Lakeland Ginger Fingers

6oz plain flour
½ teaspoon bicarbonate of soda
1 teaspoon cream of tartar
1 teaspoon ground ginger
pinch of nutmeg
2oz oats
6oz butter
4oz brown sugar

Sift together the flour, bicarbonate of soda, cream of tartar and spices. Stir in the oats and rub in the butter. Stir in the sugar. Press the mixture into a greased 12" x 8" tin and level the top.

Bake for 30 minutes at 325°. Cut into fingers and leave to cool.

The narrow streets of Hawkshead make it one of Lakeland's most attractive villages. It is possible to visit the old school where Wordsworth was a pupil. (Walt Unsworth)

Coconut Oat Cookies

4oz plain flour
2oz coconut
2oz oats
3oz caster sugar
4oz butter
1 tablespoon syrup
½ teaspoon bicarbonate of soda dissolved in
1 tablespoon hot water
1 teaspoon vanilla essence

Mix flour, coconut, oats and sugar into a large bowl.
Heat the butter and syrup gently in a pan until the butter just melts.
Pour the melted butter and syrup on to the flour mixture, add the dissolved bicarbonate of soda and vanilla essence. Stir with a palette knife, until the mixture resembles fine breadcrumbs. With your fingers gather together into a dough.
Shape into small balls and place on to a greased baking sheet. Flatten slightly and press a ¼ cherry on to each one.
Bake for 15-20 minutes at 350° until a cookie, lifted carefully, is lightly brown underneath.

***

Hawkshead Biscuits

1lb S.R. flour
1 oz caster sugar
1 beaten egg
3oz butter
pinch of salt
½ pint of milk

Rub the butter into the flour, add the sugar and salt, mix to a light dough with the egg and milk. Roll out to about ½ " thick, cut into rounds. Prick all over with a fork, place on a greased baking sheet and bake at 350° for 10 minutes or until lightly golden.

Oaten Date Crisps

4oz wholewheat flour
6oz oats
8oz margarine
8oz chopped dates
2 tablespoons water
2 teaspoons lemon juice
1oz soft brown sugar
pinch of cinnamon

Mix the flour and oats together, rub in the fat. Turn out on to a lightly floured board and knead until smooth. Cut into half and press half into a well greased 7" square tin.

Simmer dates with the water until soft. Cool, and stir in the lemon juice, sugar and cinnamon. Spread this mixture over the dough. Cover with the other half of the dough. Smooth the top and bake at 350° for 25 minutes. Cut into squares while warm. Apples can be used instead of dates.

***

Ginger Nuts

8oz S.R. flour
4oz caster sugar
2 teaspoons ground ginger
1 teaspoon bicarbonate of soda
2 tablespoons golden syrup
2 tablespoons black treacle
3oz margarine
1 egg

Sieve all the dry ingredients into a bowl. Heat the margarine, syrup and treacle gently. When the margarine has melted remove from the heat and add beaten egg. Pour this on to the dry ingredients and beat well. Leave to cool slightly. Roll into small balls made from a heaped teaspoon of the mixture. Place them, well apart, on a greased baking sheet. Bake at 325° for 15-20 minutes. Leave to cool before removing the biscuits, as they will harden as they cool.

Oatmeal Cookies

3oz butter
8oz soft brown sugar
2 beaten eggs
1 egg yolk
1 teaspoon vanilla essence
6oz flour
½ teaspoon salt
½ teaspoon baking powder
6oz oatmeal soaked in 2 fluid oz. milk

Cream the butter and sugar, add the eggs and extra yolk. Beat well, mix in vanilla essence. Sift the flour, salt and baking powder, carefully fold this into the mixture. Fold in the oatmeal and mix until smooth. Drop teaspoonfuls of the mixture onto a greased baking sheet, sprinkle with soft brown sugar. Bake at 350° for about 10 minutes.

***

Judith's Crunchies

4oz S.R. flour
2oz oats
4oz margarine
3oz sugar
1 teaspoon syrup
3 teaspoons boiling water
few drops of vanilla essence

Cream the margarine and sugar. Add the syrup, water and vanilla essence, flour and oats.

Roll into small balls, place on a greased baking sheet, flatten slightly. Bake at 300°-325° for 20 minutes until a golden colour.

*The high and lonely hamlet of Watendlath, above Borrowdale
was the setting for Sir Hugh Walpole's novel, Judith Paris.
(Walt Unsworth)*

Ginger Scrunchies

4oz butter
3oz sugar
3oz golden syrup
8oz plain flour
pinch of salt
2 teaspoons ground ginger
2oz oats
1 teaspoon bicarbonate of soda
a little water

Heat the butter, sugar and syrup in a pan. Sieve the flour, salt and ginger, add the oats. Dissolve the bicarbonate of soda in a little water, add this to the flour mixture and then mix in the warmed syrup.

Form into small balls, place on a greased baking sheet and bake at 325° until golden brown about 15-20 minutes.

Keep in an airtight tin.

***

Ginger Flapjack

Base:-	*Topping:-*
4oz margarine	*2oz margarine*
8oz oats	*4 tablespoons icing sugar*
3oz soft brown sugar	*½ teaspoon ground ginger*
1 teaspoon ground ginger	*2 tablespoons golden syrup*
1 tablespoon golden syrup	
1 tablespoon clear honey	

Mix together the oats, sugar and the ground ginger in a large bowl.

Melt the margarine with the syrup and the honey over a low heat, stirring all the time. Stir the melted mixture into the oats, Mix well. Grease an 8″ square cake tin, turn the mixture into the tin and press it down with a knife.

Bake at 350° for 20 minutes. Do not overcook.

Prepare the topping. Melt the margarine over a low heat, remove from the heat and add the icing sugar, ground ginger and the syrup. Pour the topping over the cooled flapjack and leave to set. When cold cut into squares.

Cherry and Chocolate Chip Chews

8oz butter
4oz caster sugar
4 tablespoons condensed milk
12oz self-raising flour
4oz chocolate, broken into small chips
4oz chopped cherries

Cream the butter and sugar, mix in all the other ingredients. Roll into small walnut sized balls and place on to a greased baking sheet. Bake at 350° for 15 minutes.

***

Millom Yo-Yo's

6oz S.R. flour
3oz butter
3oz sugar
1 beaten egg
1 tablespoon cocoa

Cream the butter and sugar, add egg, mix well. Add the flour and cocoa. Blend well. Roll into small ball shapes. Put onto a greased baking tray, flatten slightly. Bake at 350° for 20 minutes. Sandwich together with chocolate butter cream. Decorate with a little melted chocolate.

***

Lemon Crunch Fingers

6oz shortcrust pastry
apricot jam
3oz butter
3oz golden syrup
1oz soft brown sugar
4oz oats
2 tablespoons lemon juice

Line a greased swiss-roll tin with the pastry, spread with the apricot jam.

Gently warm the butter, sugar and syrup until the butter has melted. Stir in the oats and lemon juice. Pour this mixture over the jam. Bake at 375° for 25 minutes until golden brown.

Cool and cut into fingers.

Potato Biscuits

4oz plain flour
1 teaspoon salt
4oz rolled oats
2oz sugar
3oz butter
4oz cold mashed potato

Put the flour, salt and rolled oats into a bowl, stir in the sugar and rub in the butter. Knead in the mashed potato until a stiff dough is formed. Roll out on to a floured board to about ⅛" thick. Cut into rounds with a 3" pastry cutter. Place on to a greased baking sheet and bake at 325° until the biscuits are crisp but not brown, about 15-20 minutes. Lift carefully on to a wire rack to cool.

To make a savoury biscuit to eat with cheese, just omit the sugar.

***

Lakeland Shortcake

½lb plain flour
¼lb soft brown sugar
¼ teaspoon bicarbonate of soda
¼lb butter
½ teaspoon ground ginger

Sift all the dry ingredients into a bowl, rub in the butter. Grease and line with paper a swiss-roll tin. Place the mixture into the tin and level off, press down with the fingers. Bake at 350° until brown, about 30 minutes. Remove from the oven. Allow to cool for 5 minutes and then cut into two whilst still hot.

Filling:-
4oz icing sugar
2oz butter
½ teaspoon ground ginger
2oz of preserved ginger
1 teaspoon of the ginger syrup

Make the filling by creaming the butter and sugar, add the ginger and syrup. Use to sandwich the two halves of shortcake together.

Rowan berries in the Kentmere valley. (Walt Unsworth)

Rhubarb Shortcake

Take a few sticks of rhubarb and cook in a casserole in the oven with a tablespoon of water and a little sugar until tender, but not broken.

Shortcake:

12oz plain flour

4oz margarine

2oz sugar

1 egg

1 teaspoon baking powder

milk to mix

Rub the margarine into the flour, add all the dry ingredients, mix egg into the mixture and add enough milk to make a stiff dough. Divide into two. Roll out one half into an oblong shape, ¼ inch thick. Place onto a greased baking tin. Spread with cooled, cooked rhubarb. Roll out other half to fit over the top. Bake at 400° for 25 minutes. When cold cut into slices.

***

Chocolate Caramel Shortcake

Base:

8oz plain flour

3oz caster sugar

6oz margarine

Caramel:

4oz margarine

2 tablespoons syrup

4oz caster sugar

1 small tin of condensed milk

Make the base by mixing the flour and sugar, rub in the margarine and form into a ball. Spread this evenly onto a well greased swiss-roll tin. Bake at 350° until light brown. Leave to cool.

Make the caramel, place all the ingredients into a heavy bottomed pan. Bring to the boil, boil for 5 minutes stirring all the time. Pour over the base, spread evenly and leave to cool.

Cover with melted chocolate, cut into fingers when cold.

Chocolate Fruit and Nut Bar

1 large tin condensed milk
4oz oats
2oz coconut
3oz sultanas
2oz chopped dates
2oz glacé cherries
1oz chopped walnuts
chocolate, melted to cover

Mix all the ingredients together. Place into a deep oblong, well greased tin. Bake at 300° for about 30 minutes or until coloured on top.

When cool, cover with melted chocolate.

***

Oatmeal Parkin

Lovely when freshly baked, but if you can manage to keep it in an airtight tin for a week or two, it then becomes wonderful and chewy.

6oz medium oatmeal	*3oz margarine*
3oz self-raising flour	*3oz soft brown sugar*
pinch of salt	*1½ teaspoons ground ginger*
4oz golden syrup	*1 beaten egg*
1oz black treacle	*1 dessertspoon milk*

Put the syrup, treacle, margarine and sugar into a saucepan and place over a gentle heat until the margarine has melted, do not over heat.

Meanwhile place the oatmeal, flour and ginger into a mixing bowl, add salt and then gradually stir in the warmed syrup mixture until everything is blended. Add the beaten egg and milk.

Grease a 6″ square baking tin and pour in the mixture, bake in the centre of the oven, 275° for about 1½ hours, it should feel springy when cooked. Cool in tin for 30 minutes. Don't worry if it sinks in the middle. It will still taste good.

Oatmeal Gingerbread

6oz plain flour
½ teaspoon bicarbonate of soda
3oz margarine
6oz medium oatmeal
1½ teaspoons ground ginger

3oz dark brown sugar
1 egg
2oz black treacle
½ pint sour milk

Sift the flour and bicarbonate of soda, rub in margarine: stir in oatmeal, ginger and sugar.

Make a well in the centre, add the egg, treacle and half the milk.

Gradually draw in the dry ingredients until all is blended and then add the rest of the milk. Put the mixture into a well greased and lightly floured large loaf tin. Bake at 350° for about 55 minutes or until just firm in the centre. Leave in the tin for 15 minutes to cool. Keep for at least three days before cutting.

***

Sticky Gingerbread

8oz butter
8oz soft brown sugar
8oz black treacle
12oz plain flour
2 beaten eggs
2 level dessertspoons ground ginger
1 level dessertspoon ground cinnamon
pinch of salt
2 level teaspoons bicarbonate of soda
½ pint warm milk

Grease and line an 8" square tin.

Melt together, over a low heat, the treacle, sugar and butter stirring all the time. Remove from the heat and stir in the beaten eggs. Sieve the dry ingredients into a bowl and stir in the melted mixture. Put the bicarbonate of soda into a small bowl and pour the warm milk over it, add this to the other mixture.

Pour into the prepared tin and bake at 300° for about 1½ hours. You may have to cover the surface with greased paper after an hour to prevent the surface from over cooking. This gingerbread improves with keeping.

In Autumn the Lake District turns to gold. A scene by the banks of the River Rothay near Ambleside. (Walt Unsworth)

Apple Gingerbread Cake

For the Topping:
2oz of softened butter
4 tablespoons soft brown sugar
2 tart dessert apples,
cored and sliced

For the Cake:
4oz S.R. flour
½ teaspoon salt
1½ teaspoon ground ginger
½ teaspoon grated nutmeg
4oz butter
4oz soft brown sugar
juice of 1 lemon
2 large eggs

Make the topping, cream together the butter and the sugar, spread the mixture on to the base of a greased 8 inch sandwich tin. Arrange the apple slices evenly over the mixture.

To make the cake, sift together the flour, salt and spices. In another bowl cream the butter and the sugar until fluffy, add the lemon juice. Beat in the eggs and then fold in the flour and the spices. Spread the mixture over the apples. Bake at 350° for 45 minutes. Turn out on to a serving dish.

***

Grasmere Gingerbread

There are many variations of Grasmere Gingerbread. The original can only be bought at the little shop in Grasmere where the recipe is a closely guarded secret.

This is the recipe I use:-
8oz fine oatmeal
4oz soft brown sugar
1 teaspoon ground ginger
¼ teaspoon baking powder
4oz butter

Sift the ginger and baking powder into the oatmeal, mix well. Melt the butter over a low heat. Mix the sugar into the oatmeal and then bind everything together with the melted butter. Press the mixture into an oblong tin, bake until golden brown, about 30-35 minutes at 350°. Mark into pieces when warm but leave in the tin until cold.

Border Gingerbread

6oz rolled oats
6oz light brown sugar
6oz S.R. flour
6oz margarine
6oz black treacle
4 teaspoons ground ginger
2 teaspoons ground cinnamon
1 teaspoon salt
6oz sultanas
3 eggs
½ pint milk

Heat the margarine and treacle gently just until the margarine has melted. Remove from heat and when cool stir in eggs and milk. Sift the flour and spices into a bowl, stir in the oats, sugar and sultanas. Pour in the treacle mixture and mix well. Pour into a greased and lined 10″ square tin and bake in the centre of the oven at 350° for about 1¼ hours. The cake should be shrinking away from the sides of the tin when cooked. Leave to cool in the tin for a few minutes. This gingerbread will improve if kept wrapped for 2-3 days before cutting.

***

Light Ginger Cake

6oz margarine
6oz light soft brown sugar
8oz plain flour
1 teaspoon baking powder
2 teaspoon ground ginger
½ teaspoon ground cinnamon
3oz chopped peel
3 beaten eggs

Cream the margarine and sugar, gradually add the eggs. Sift the flour and spices and fold in with the chopped peel. Grease a 2lb loaf tin, spoon in the mixture and bake at 350° for about 50-60 minutes. Leave to cool in the tin and then turn out on to a wire tray.

Buttermere, backed by Fleetwith Pike, where the steep profile of Honister Crag is seen above Gatesgarthdale.
There is a delightful lakeside footpath which makes a fine circular walk from Buttermere.

(Walt Unsworth)

73

Fell-Top Cake

12oz crushed digestive biscuits
6oz margarine
6oz sultanas and raisins
1½oz sugar
3oz syrup
1½oz cocoa

Melt syrup, margarine and sugar. Add the dried fruit and biscuits, mix well, add cocoa. Put into a greased shallow tin. Allow to cool and then cover with melted chocolate.

***

Almond Slice

Line a greased swiss-roll tin with short-crust pastry. Spread with raspberry jam.

Topping:-
4oz margarine
4oz caster sugar
6oz oats
1 beaten egg
1 teaspoon almond essence

Melt the margarine and sugar over a low heat in a medium sized saucepan.
Remove from heat, add all the other ingredients and mix well.
Spread evenly over the jam, sprinkle with flaked almonds.
Bake at 330° for 25 minutes.

Cinnamon Tea Cake

8oz plain flour
½ teaspoon salt
1½ teaspoons baking powder
3oz margarine
3oz caster sugar
1 egg, beaten
¼ pint of milk

Sieve the flour, salt and baking powder into a bowl. Rub in the margarine and add the sugar. Mix all to a soft batter using the beaten egg and milk. Turn into an 8″ greased tin.

Cinnamon Topping:-
1oz flour
2oz caster sugar
½ teaspoon ground cinnamon
1½oz margarine

Put the flour, sugar and cinnamon in a bowl and rub in the margarine. Sprinkle over the mixture in the cake tin.

Bake at 375° for 35-40 minutes.

***

Lakeland Fruit Cake

A great favourite for that special occasion.

3 teacups dessicated coconut
1 cup chopped dates
1 cup chopped walnuts
1 cup raisins
1 cup glacé cherries

1 cup of mixed peel and ginger
1 cup chopped dried apricots
1½ cups condensed milk
teaspoon vanilla essence

Mix all the ingredients together in a large bowl. Line an 8″ cake tin with greased paper and pack the mixture in well. Decorate the top with a few extra cherries, half walnuts and thin slices of peel. Bake in a slow oven, 280°- 300° for 1½-2 hours.

When cold, wrap in foil and store for about 4 weeks to 'ripen'. Do not be tempted to cut beforehand as the longer you keep the cake the better it becomes.

Westmorland Spice Cake

3 eggs
6oz caster sugar
10 fluid oz clear honey
4oz chopped almonds
grated rind of ½ orange
grated rind of ½ lemon
2oz mixed peel

10oz plain flour
1 teaspoon baking powder
¼ teaspoon ground cloves
¼ teaspoon grated nutmeg
½ teaspoon ground cinnamon

In a large mixing bowl, beat the eggs and sugar until pale and fluffy.

Stir in the honey, almonds, lemon and orange rind and mixed peel. Sift in the flour, baking powder and all the spices. Stir until thoroughly mixed.

Grease a shallow 8" square cake tin. Spoon the mixture into the tin. Place in the centre of the oven and bake at 375° for 40-45 minutes. Allow to cool in the tin for 15 minutes before turning out.

This cake can be iced but is delicious sliced and spread with butter.

***

Shearing Cake

This cake was always made to celebrate the end of sheep-shearing time.

8oz plain flour
4oz butter
6oz soft brown sugar
rind of ½ lemon
1 teapoon baking powder
2 teaspoons caraway seeds
ground nutmeg
¼ pint of milk
1 egg, beaten

Rub the butter into the sifted flour and baking powder, until it is like fine breadcrumbs. Stir in the sugar, lemon rind, caraway seeds and ¼ teaspoon ground nutmeg. Mix in the milk and the beaten egg. Grease and line a 7" baking tin. Spoon in the mixture.

Bake at 350° for 1 hour.

Cumberland Courting Cake

This is a cake which is said to have been baked by young girls and given to their boy-friends on 'fair' days.

Line a swiss-roll tin with short crust pastry, cover this with a layer of sweetened cooked apple. Cream together 2oz of butter with 2 oz of sugar and then add 1 egg. Add lightly, 2oz of S.R. flour. Spread this sponge mixture over the apple and cook in a moderate oven about 35 minutes, or until firm to touch. When cold spread glacé icing over the top and cut into squares.

***

Westmorland Rum Cake

This is a lovely rich cake, useful for any special occasion. The fruit is soaked in the rum and sherry for 3 days, for a really rich flavour.

In a large bowl place,

8oz raisins	*8oz chopped dates*
8oz currants	*3oz glacé cherries*

pour over 10 fluid oz of rum and 5 fluid oz of sherry. Leave to soak for 3 days.

8oz butter	*½ teaspoon mixed spice*
12oz plain flour	*½ teaspoon cinnamon*
1 teaspoon bicarbonate of soda	*¼ teaspoon nutmeg*
1 teaspoon baking-powder	*8oz sugar*
4 eggs	

Into a large bowl sift the flour with the bicarbonate of soda, baking-powder and all the spices.

In another bowl cream the butter and the sugar until light in colour.

Beat in the eggs one at a time, fold in half of the flour mixture. Stir in all the fruit mixture. Fold in the remaining flour mixture until all is mixed well. Grease well an 8″ round tin, spoon in the cake mix and hollow out the top of the cake so that it will rise evenly.

Bake at 300° for 2-2½ hours. Remove from the tin and allow to cool. Wrap in foil and keep for at least two weeks before cutting.

Westmorland Dream Cake

4oz butter
4oz plain flour
1oz soft brown sugar

Rub the fat into the flour and add the brown sugar. Put into a greased swiss-roll tin, flatten out the mixture and bake for 20 minutes at 350°. Cool in tin.

8oz soft brown sugar
1oz plain flour
4oz chopped walnuts
3oz coconut
½ level teaspoon baking powder
pinch of salt

Mix all these together and then add 2 beaten eggs.

Mix well, spread on top of the cooked mixture and bake for 20 minutes. Do not overcook, as cake will harden as it cools.

***

Applesauce Cake

8oz plain flour
¼ teaspoon salt
1 teaspoon baking-powder
1 teaspoon ground cinnamon
½ teaspoon ground cloves
6oz soft brown sugar

4oz softened butter
3 eggs
4oz raisins
4oz chopped walnuts
8oz of 'made' applesauce

Sift the flour with the salt and all the spices. Cream the butter and sugar together, add the eggs one by one, continue to beat until smooth. Add the flour mixture a little at a time, stir well. Add the raisins, walnuts and the apple sauce. Mix well.

Grease an 8½" cake tin and dust with a little flour.

Pour the mixture into a cake tin and bake at 350° for 1¼-1½ hours, or until a skewer placed in the centre of the cake comes out clean.

Ennerdale Cake

1lb S.R. flour
pinch of salt
4oz caster sugar
4oz butter
4oz lard
2 beaten eggs
water to mix
raspberry jam

Sift the flour and salt, rub in butter and lard. Mix in sugar. Add eggs and enough water to mix to a firm pastry. Roll out on a floured board, divide into half. Line a greased swiss-roll tin with one portion of the pastry, spread with raspberry jam and cover with second portion of pastry. Sprinkle with caster sugar.
Bake at 350° for 20 minutes or until just slightly golden brown.

*****

Coconut Meringue

To make base:
3oz margarine
4oz caster sugar
6oz S.R. flour
½ teaspoon salt
2 egg yolks, 2 tablespoons milk.

Cream margarine with the sugar, beat in egg yolks and fold in all the other ingredients, add milk. Spread this mixture into a greased swiss-roll tin.

Topping:
2 stiffly beaten egg whites
2oz coconut
4oz caster sugar
1oz chopped nuts
1oz chopped glacé cherries

Mix all the ingredients into the egg whites gently. Spread over the base. Bake at 350° for 20-25 minutes.

Caraway Seed Cake

This was a firm favourite with Dorothy Wordsworth and was perhaps served with afternoon tea at Dove Cottage.

6oz margarine
6oz caster sugar
8oz plain flour
3 eggs, beaten
1 teaspoon baking powder
pinch of salt
1 tablespoon ground almonds
3 teaspoons caraway seeds
1 tablespoon milk

Cream the margarine and sugar until light in colour. Gradually beat in the eggs and the caraway seeds. Fold in the sifted flour, baking powder, salt and ground almonds with the milk. Grease a 2lb loaf tin and spoon in the mixture. Bake at 350° for 45-55 minutes. Leave to cool in tin before turning out.

***

Paradise Cake

Shortcrust Pastry:-
4oz margarine
3oz caster sugar
2 eggs
2oz S.R. flour
2oz ground almonds
6oz mixed fruit
raspberry jam

Line a greased swiss-roll tin with pastry. Cream together the margarine and sugar, beat in 2 eggs, add flour, ground almonds and mixed fruit. Spread jam over pastry, cover with the creamed mixture and bake at 350° until set, about 40 minutes.

Dramatic light on Dow Crag, Coniston; a favourite climbing crag.
(Walt Unsworth)

Lemon Cake

Cake:-
8oz butter
8oz sugar
grated rind and juice of 1 lemon
4 eggs
8oz S.R. flour

Icing:-
4oz butter
10oz icing sugar, sifted
grated rind of 1 lemon
3 tablespoons lemon juice
2 drops of yellow colouring

Filling:-
Lemon Curd

Beat the butter and sugar together until light and fluffy, add the lemon rind and juice, beat until smooth.

Add the eggs one at a time with one tablespoon of flour with each egg. Beat them in well. Sift in the remaining flour, fold in well. Grease two sandwich tins and pour in the cake mixture. Bake at 350° for 30 to 35 minutes.

Make the icing by creaming the sugar and butter together, add the lemon rind, juice and food colouring. Beat until the mixture is smooth.

Split the sandwich cakes into two and spread with lemon curd, making a cake of four layers. Spread the icing over the sides and top. Decorate with sugared lemon slices.

***

Super Apple Cake

4oz margarine
4oz sugar
4oz S.R. flour
2 eggs
grated rind of lemon
2 large cooking apples, peeled and sliced
milk to mix

2 teaspoons cinnamon
and 2 tablespoons of sugar
(mixed together)
1oz of butter

Beat the margarine and sugar to a cream, add eggs, flour and lemon rind. Mix with enough milk to a stiff consistency. Put into a greased, floured 8 inch cake tin. Place layers of apple slices on top. Sprinkle cinnamon and sugar mixture over the apples and finish off with the butter cut into small pieces. Bake at 400° for 35-40 minutes.

Serve with cream when cold.

Pastry Cake

A very rich fruit cake. Keep wrapped for at least two weeks before cutting.

Filling:-

8oz plain flour	12oz sultanas
1 teaspoon bicarbonate of soda	12oz currants
1½ teaspoons baking powder	4oz chopped almonds
4oz soft brown sugar	4oz chopped walnuts
1 teaspoon mixed spice	4oz mixed peel
½ teaspoon ground cinnamon	grated rind and juice of 1 lemon
½ teaspoon ground ginger	6 fluid oz milk
¼ teaspoon ground mace	1 tablespoon rum

Pastry:-

12oz plain flour	2 beaten eggs
¼ teaspoon salt	water to mix
3oz butter	2 tablespoons sugar

1 beaten egg, to brush pastry with

Make the pastry: sift the flour and salt together, rub in the butter until it resembles fine breadcrumbs. Mix in the sugar. Add the beaten egg with 4 tablespoons of cold water, mix into the flour with a knife. Add more water if the mixture is too dry. Chill while you mix the cake filling.

Sift the flour and salt, stir in all the dry ingredients. Pour in the lemon juice, milk and rum. Set aside.

Grease a 7″ cake tin.

Divide the dough into ⅔rds and ⅓ portions keeping the smaller portion to cover the top. Roll out the larger piece into a circle about ½″ thick. Carefully lift the dough and line the bottom and sides of the cake tin, trim off any excess.

Spoon the cake filling into the tin, pressing flat with the back of a spoon. Roll out the remaining dough into a circle large enough to cover the top of the tin. Dampen the edges of the dough and press together to form a seal.

Brush the top with the beaten egg.

Bake for 15 minutes at 400° then remove from the oven, cover with foil, reduce the oven temperature to 325° and continue to cook for 3½ hours.

Remove from the oven and carefully turn out of the tin to cool.

Rhubarb Cake

2oz butter
12oz rhubarb, cut into 2" lengths
5oz sugar
2 teaspoons lemon rind, grated
½ teaspoon ground ginger
¼ teaspoon grated nutmeg
6oz flour
½ teaspoon baking powder
¼ teaspoon salt
2 eggs beaten with 4 tablespoons milk
2 tablespoons lemon juice

Grease well an 8" square tin, arrange the rhubarb in the tin.

Mix 4oz of the sugar with the lemon rind, ginger, nutmeg and 1 tablespoon of the flour. Sprinkle this mixture over the rhubarb.

Sift the remaining flour with the baking-powder and salt. Add the butter and rub in until the mixture resembles breadcrumbs. Add the egg and milk mixture with the lemon juice, mix well until smooth and looks like a thick batter. Spoon it over the rhubarb in the tin.

Bake for 40 minutes at 350°, a skewer inserted into the centre of the cake should come out clean. Allow to cool. Place a serving dish over the cake and turn out. Serve warm.

***

Overnight Spice Cake

1lb plain flour
8oz butter
8oz caster sugar
4oz ground almonds
2 teaspoons mixed spice
2½ teaspoons bicarbonate of soda
8oz currants
8oz raisins
½ pint sour milk

Rub the butter into the flour until the mixture resembles fine breadcrumbs. Sift in the spice and bicarbonate of soda. Mix in the sugar and ground almonds. Stir in the dried fruit. Mix to a soft dough with the sour milk. Grease and line with paper an 8" round cake tin. Place the mixture into the tin and leave to stand overnight. Next day bake at 325° for 1 hour, reduce the heat to 300° and bake for a further 1½ hours. Cool on a wire rack.

Old Fashioned Nut and Apple Cake

Cake:
6oz butter
3 large eggs
5oz S.R. flour
1oz cocoa
6oz caster sugar
4oz ground hazel-nuts

Filling:
1lb cooking apples
juice of ½ lemon
2oz caster sugar

Topping:
4oz plain chocolate
1 teaspoon oil
2 tablespoons cold water
1oz caster sugar

Grease and line a 7 inch deep tin, also grease the paper.

Beat the butter and sugar, add the eggs, hazelnuts flour and cocoa. Turn mixture into tin and hollow out the centre slightly. Bake at 375° for 40-45 minutes. Prepare apple filling by cooking apples to a pulp with the lemon juice and sugar. Allow to cool.

Split cake in half and fill with the apple mixture. To make topping, melt all the ingredients in a bowl over a pan of hot water, pour over the cake and allow to trickle over the sides.

***

Luscious Chocolate Cake

So rich and sticky but so simple to make, it requires no cooking.

Melt 8oz of cooking chocolate in a dish over a pan of simmering water, stirring until it is soft and sticky. Let it cool slightly, then stir in 5 egg yolks, 4oz caster sugar, 4 oz melted butter, then the 5 egg whites whipped absolutely stiff. Dip 8oz of boudoir biscuits quickly into very strong coffee and press them round the sides and over the bottom of a round cake tin. Because they are wet they will stick.

Pour in the chocolate mixture. Cover with a small plate. Put a weight on top and chill it for 24 hours. Turn out and garnish with fresh cream and grated chocolate.

Lakeland Bake

Make 8oz of shortcrust pastry, roll out half and line a greased swiss-roll tin.

Filling:-
8oz of cake crumbs
3oz mixed peel
2oz raisins
1 tablespoon lemon juice
4 tablespoons golden syrup
4 tablespoons milk
Milk and caster sugar to glaze

Mix all these ingredients together and spoon onto the pastry in the tin. Roll out the rest of the pastry and cover the filling. Seal the edges. Brush the top with milk and sprinkle with caster sugar.

Bake for 45 minutes at 375° until golden brown. Allow to cool and then cut into fingers.

***

Queen Elizabeth I Cake

This is not a 'Lakeland' recipe but a traditional 'Olde English'. It has proved to be extremely popular in Brockhole Cafe.

Base:-
1 cup boiling water
1 cup chopped dates
1 teaspoon bicarbonate of soda
¼ cup margarine
1½ cups of plain flour
1 cup sugar
½ cup chopped nuts
½ teaspoon salt,
1 teaspoon baking powder
1 teaspoon vanilla essence
1 beaten egg

Pour boiling water over the dates and bicarbonate of soda. Rub the margarine into the flour, add the sugar, chopped nuts, baking powder and salt. Add the vanilla essence and the beaten egg to the dates and then add this mixture to the flour mix. Mix to a soft batter.

Turn into a greased and paper-lined swiss-roll tin, bake at 325° for about 35 minutes. Allow to go cold.

Icing:-
2 tablespoons margarine
5 tablespoons soft brown sugar
5 tablespoons single cream

Mix all these ingredients in a saucepan and boil until it begins to thicken. Spread over the cooked base and sprinkle with toasted chopped almonds.

Cut into squares when set.

***

Lyth Valley Damson Cheese

3lb damsons
granulated sugar

Wash fruit, place into a pan and cover with water. Simmer over a low heat until damsons are quite soft. Rub through a sieve with a wooden spoon and measure the resulting pulp. Allow 1lb of granulated sugar to each pint of pulp. Return the pulp and sugar to a preserving pan and stir over a gentle heat until all the sugar is dissolved. Boil for 40-45 minutes, making sure that you stir the bottom of the pan to avoid the pulp sticking, until the cheese begins to thicken.

Remove from the heat, pour into small clean warm jars and cover as for jam. Delicious with Lakeland Ginger Scones.

***

Damson and Apple Jam

3lb damsons
1 pint water
3lb cooking apples
6lb granulated sugar
knob of butter

Place damsons and water in a preserving pan, cover and simmer over a low heat until the fruit is soft. Meanwhile peel, core and chop the apples.

When damsons are soft, sieve and return the pulp to the pan with the apples. Cover and simmer until the apples are soft, about 20 minutes. Measure all the pulp and add 1lb of sugar to every pint of pulp. Return to the pan, over a low heat dissolve the sugar, add a knob of butter. Bring to the boil and boil rapidly for about 5 minutes, stirring occasionally until setting point is reached. Using a sugar thermometer this is 104°C. Let the jam stand for 5-10 minutes before pouring into jars.

***

Damson blossom in the Lyth Valley.
Any Cumbrian will tell you that the best damsons in Britain come from this valley! (Walt Unsworth)

Cumberland Rum Butter

½lb butter, melted
1lb of soft brown sugar
half a grated nutmeg
wineglass of rum

Mix the sugar, nutmeg and rum together, pour the melted butter over and mix well. Put into a bowl and leave to set.

***

Lemon Curd

Lemon curd is very easy to make and has so many uses. It will only keep for a few months and should be kept in a cool place.

12oz butter, in small pieces
2lb caster sugar
juice of six lemons and finely pared rind
8 beaten eggs

Place a large heatproof mixing bowl over a saucepan half filled with hot water. Put the butter, sugar, lemon rind and juice in the bowl. Set the pan over a low heat. Cook the mixture, stirring all the time with a wooden spoon, until the sugar has dissolved. Whisk in the eggs. Continue cooking for 35 to 40 minutes, stirring until the mixture thickens.

Remove pan from heat and carefully lift off the bowl. With a spoon lift out the lemon rind. Pour the curd into clean, warm, dry jars. Cover with greaseproof paper.

***